The Law of Attraction for Kids

Using Affirmations to Build Self-Esteem
By Jennifer Quaggin

ISBN: 1480192198
ISBN 13: 9781480192195
Library of Congress Control Number: 2012920792
CreateSpace Independent Publishing Platform
North Charleston, South Carolina

This book is dedicated to Evan and Fiona... and to awesome kids everywhere

The Secret to an Awesome Life

The Law of Attraction

You can be anything you want to be. That's the truth. In fact, it's the Law... the LAW OF ATTRACTION.

Over 40,000 years ago, people knew about this Law and used it to heal people who were sick and to make crops grow. They could even use it to change the weather and to stop natural disasters from happening. These people were called Shamans. Since then, hundreds of people have written about this Law and, today, high-achievers around the world use it to bring themselves friends, happiness, success, good luck, and money.

This Law is something you can use too to bring yourself anything you want in life, to help you to become anything you want to be. And the great news is that it's easy to use!

The first thing you have to do is get rid of unhappy thoughts. Then, you have to fill your head with happy thoughts. This book will help you to do that.

If you read the chapters "Saying Good-Bye to Unhappy Thoughts" and "Thinking Happy Thoughts" every day for 21 days, you'll soon find that wonderful things start happening in your life. And if you keep on reading those two chapters every day after the 21 days are up, things will only get better!

Not all of the Happy Thoughts might be true yet. But if you read them and imagine what it would feel like if they were all true, then they will absolutely become true one day very soon. That's the way the Law of Attraction works.

So, are you ready to have an amazing life? Are you ready to find out just what an awesome person you really are?

I hope so
because by reading this –
guess what? – you've already started!

Saying Good-bye
to Unhappy
Thoughts

Saying Good-Bye to Feeling Bad

I say good-bye forever to thinking that I'm not perfect. I was born perfect. I will always be perfect.

I say good-bye forever to thinking that my dreams are stupid or that they won't come true. My dreams are exactly what they're supposed to be and will absolutely come true!

I say good-bye forever to thinking that I can't have a happy, wonderful life. I was born to have a happy, wonderful life. I deserve to have one and I WILL have one... starting today!

I say good-bye forever to thinking that school is hard.
When I study, school gets easy for me!

I say good-bye forever to thinking that I can't do well in school.
I can do great in school... and at everything I try!

I say good-bye forever to thinking that people don't like me.
Everyone likes me!

I say good-bye forever to thinking that I don't look good
or that my body isn't right. I look great! When I think
I look great, other people think I look great too!

I say good-bye forever to thinking that I shouldn't tell an adult when someone is hurting me. Telling is the right thing to do, no matter who is hurting me. Telling makes me a hero because it stops something bad from happening. It means I'm brave, strong, and courageous and can stand up for myself.

I say good-bye forever to anything mean or hurtful anyone has ever said or done to me. I don't deserve to have mean or hurtful things said or done to me. I don't believe any mean things that are said about me... because they're not true! They were said to make me feel bad about myself. I won't let them. Nothing anyone does or says can stop me from being happy or can stop me from feeling good about myself.

School

I like studying because I know that it will make me be successful at school and in life.

Everything I study is interesting to me.

Studying makes me smarter.

All of my teachers and classmates like me and I like them.

I get good grades in all of my classes.

It's okay to make mistakes. Everyone makes mistakes. Mistakes are a way of learning and of getting better.

I'm not afraid to speak up in class. I have good ideas that deserve to be heard.

I like learning. Learning is fun and exciting.

I love to learn new things. I am a fast learner. Learning is easy for me.

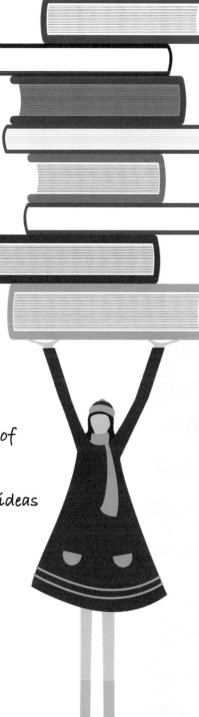

Being Healthy

I am healthy. I like eating and drinking things that are good for me.

When I exercise, it makes me feel good. It makes me happy.

I take good care of my body. I take good care of me.

I like spending some time outside every day. The fresh air makes me feel good.

I feel great!

I look great!

I AM great!

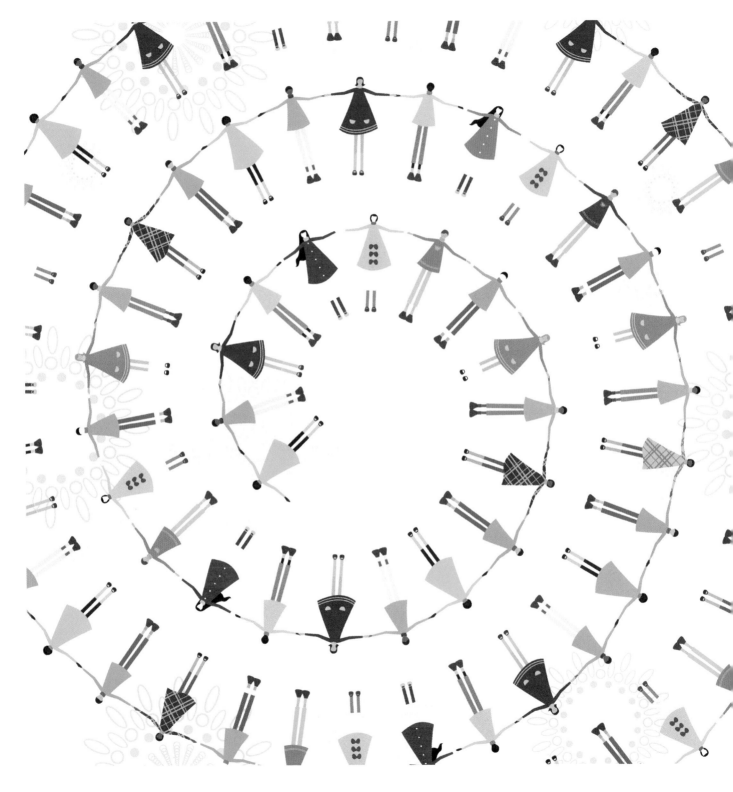

Acting Responsibly

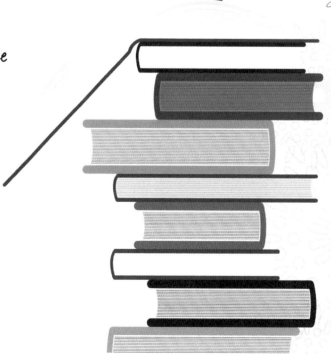

I always tell the truth. It's the right thing to do.

I am helpful. I like helping.

I am a good listener.

I always do the right thing. Doing the right thing means treating other people the way I like to be treated.

When I see somebody being picked on or hurt, I always go get help.

I like to share. Sharing makes me feel good in my heart.

I know that because somebody might be different than me doesn't make them wrong or strange or ugly. Not everybody is the same as me. It is our differences that make us special and interesting. It is our differences that make this world a beautiful place to be.

I like to learn about all kinds of ideas, customs, and beliefs. This helps me to understand other people. This helps me to be a great person.

By being nice to myself and nice to other people, I can make this world a wonderful place for everyone. I can change the world.

Liking Yourself

I am perfect just the way I am.

I came into this world to
make a difference and to be happy.

Beautiful and handsome come in all
different shapes and sizes and colors.
If I think that I'm beautiful or handsome,
other people will come to see me that way too.

I am awesome.

I am positive.

I love myself. When I love myself it is easy for me
to love other people and for other people to love me.

I am proud to be me.

I feel good about myself.

I am important.

I believe in me.

I'm a good friend to myself.

I care about myself and I care about other people, animals, and all living things.

Friends

I am popular. I am friendly.

It is easy for me to make friends.

I have lots of friends who love me.

I play well with other people.

I see the best in everyone.

I don't hurt other people. I don't say or do mean things.

Standing Up for Yourself

No one can make me feel bad about myself. I won't let them. They don't have that kind of power over me.

If someone says something mean to me, it's because there's something wrong with them. That's their problem not my problem.

If anyone tries to hurt me with their words or actions, I know that it is my right to go talk to a teacher, a counselor, or my parents about it. They will help me. I deserve to be helped and I'm not ashamed to ask for help.

Asking for help means that I'm courageous. Only brave people are strong enough to ask for help.

I don't let anyone hurt me. I don't deserve to be hurt. I deserve to be protected and loved.

I stand up for what is important to me. It doesn't matter what anyone else thinks.

Saying "no" doesn't make me wrong. It means that I am strong.

Making Your Dreams Come True

I can be anything I want to be.

Nothing is too hard for me. If I keep trying, I will be successful at whatever I do.

I like being unique. Being unique makes me special. Being unique lets me achieve great things in my life.

I am talented and smart. I have great ideas.

Every day I'm getting better and smarter.

I am great. I can do great things.

All of my dreams are special and, if I believe in them, they will all come true. I have the power to make them come true.

Being Calm

I am calm.

I don't worry about things. I know that everything is going to turn out just fine.

I don't get scared about what might happen. Today is going to be a great day. Tomorrow is going to be a great day too.

Even if something goes wrong, that's okay. When something goes wrong, it makes me stronger and smarter. In the end, I will always win.

I am safe. I am protected.

When I feel anxious, scared, or angry. I take five deep breaths and that makes me feel much better.

Being Happy

Everyone deserves to be happy. That includes me.

Today is going to be a great day.

I am happy.

I think happy thoughts.

Life is fun.

Life makes me smile and laugh.

I love being alive.

I was born to be great and to have a great life. Knowing this fills me with happiness.

I spend time every day thinking about all of the wonderful things in my life and everything that is wonderful about me. I write these things down so that I can read them over and over again and feel thankful and happy to be me.

I have a happy life. I will always have a happy life. It is what I was born to have. I choose to be happy now and forever.

I won't let anyone make me unhappy.

I am me. And nothing could be more wonderful than that.

I am AWESOME!

Get Ready...
Get Set...
GO!

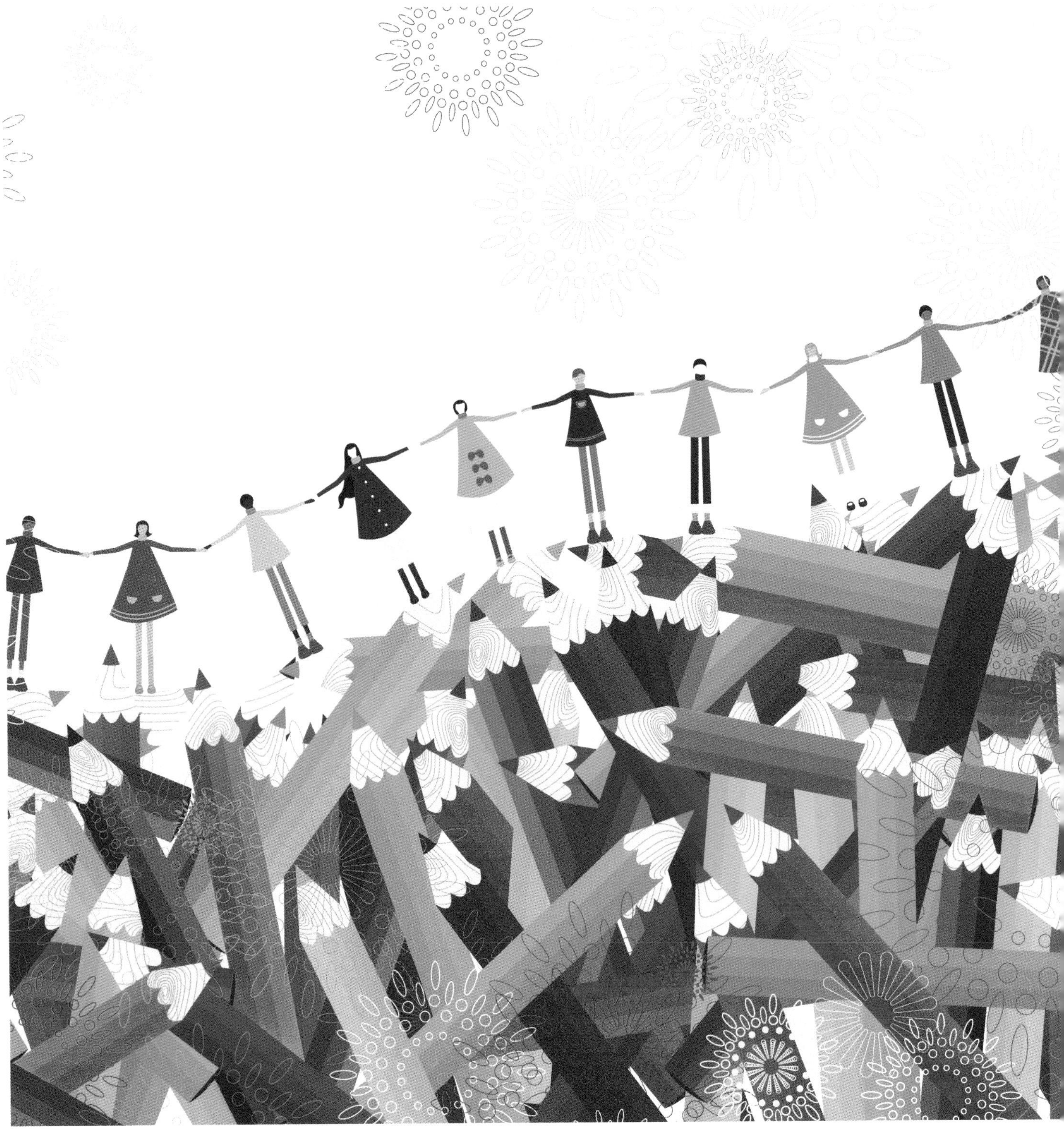

Your Awesome Life Starts Today!

You were born absolutely perfect just the way you are with everything you need to have a happy, successful, amazing life.

If you are ready to be the wonderful, awesome person you are meant to be, read this book every day for 21 days. Soon, you're going to find out that great things start happening in your life. Some of them will surprise you! Some of them will amaze you!

I'm not making this up just to make you feel good. It's the absolute, 100% truth. In fact, it's the LAW... the LAW OF ATTRACTION.

Lots of adults know about this Law and have been using it to make themselves happy, popular, rich, and successful.

You can do exactly the same thing.

All you have to do is believe.

Believe in the Law of Attraction.

Believe in yourself.

And, you know something? If you're the kind of person who would read this book all the way through to here, then you're absolutely the kind of person who is going to have an awesome life.

Guaranteed!

Acknowledgments

This book wouldn't have been possible without:

My wonderful parents who have filled my life with unconditional love since the day I was born.

My incredible family. You mean the world to me.

My amazing friend, Cindy, who was there for me when I needed a hug.

Rhonda Byrne, Esther and Jerry Hicks, Dr. Joe Vitale, Jack Canfield, Serge Kahili King, and W. Clement Stone who shared the amazing secret of the Law of Attraction with me.

Neeta Singhal and Louise L. Hay who taught me how to use affirmations to unleash the power of the Law of Attraction to quickly and easily transform my life.

Joel Osteen who taught me the meaning of true love, forgiveness, hope, and second chances.

Ellen Degeneres who made me laugh and encouraged me when the world seemed plunged in darkness.

Oprah Winfrey who inspired me with her strength and courage.

iStockphoto.com/chuwy who provided all of the fabulous artwork for the book.

Thank you from the bottom of my heart!

Printed in Great Britain
by Amazon